SHORT WALKS CORNWALL

FALMOUTH & THE LIZARD

by Phil Turner

Towanroath Engine House (Walk 1)

CONTENTS

Using this guide... 4
Route summary table 6
Map key 7
Introduction... 9
   Walking in Falmouth and The Lizard.................................. 10
   Things to see 10
   Travel 11
   Where to stay... 11

The walks

1.	St Agnes Beacon and Wheal Coates.............................	13
2.	Portreath and Tehidy Country Park	19
3.	Truro to Malpas and St Clement................................	25
4.	Gwennap Pit..	29
5.	Carn Brea	35
6.	Trelissick and Roundwood Quay	41
7.	St Mawes and St Just-in-Roseland	45
8.	Flushing to Mylor Churchtown	51
9.	Falmouth beaches and Pendennis Point	57
10.	Roseland Ramble	63
11.	Frenchman's Creek	69
12.	Penrose and Loe Bar...	75
13.	Poldhu and Halzephron Cliff...................................	81
14.	Cadgwith and the Devil's Frying Pan...........................	85
15.	Lizard Point and Church Cove..................................	91

Useful information... 95

USING THIS GUIDE

Routes in this book

In this book you will find a selection of easy or moderate walks suitable for almost everyone, including casual walkers and families with children, or for when you only have a short time to fill. The routes have been carefully chosen to allow you to explore the area and its attractions. Most routes are circular, although some linear walks may be included that use public transport to get back to the start. Although there may be some climbs there is no challenging terrain, but do bear in mind that conditions can sometimes be wet or muddy underfoot. A route summary table is included on page 6 to help you choose the right walk.

Clothing and footwear

You won't need any special equipment to enjoy these walks. The weather in Britain can be changeable, so choose clothing suitable for the season and wear or carry a waterproof jacket. For footwear, comfortable walking boots or trainers with a good grip are best. A small rucksack for drinks, snacks and spare clothing is useful. See www.adventuresmart.uk.

Walk descriptions

At the beginning of each walk you'll find all the information you need:

- start/finish location, with postcode and a what3words address to help you find it
- parking and transport information, estimated walking time, total distance and climb
- details of public toilets available along the route and where you can get refreshments
- a summary of the key highlights of the walk and what you might see

Timings given are the time to complete the walk at a reasonable walking pace. Allow extra time for extended stops or if walking with children.

The route is described in clear, easy-to-follow directions, with each waypoint marked on an accompanying map extract. It's a good idea to read the whole of the route instructions before setting out, so that you know what to expect.

Maps, GPX files and what3words

Extracts from the OS® 1:25,000 map accompany each route. GPX files for all the walks in this book are available to download at www.cicerone.co.uk/1173/gpx.

What3words is a free smartphone app which identifies every 3m square of the globe with a unique three-word address, e.g. ///destiny.cafe.sonic. For more information see https://what3words.com/products/what3words-app.

Walking with children

Even young children can be surprisingly strong walkers, but every family is different and you may need to adapt the timings given in this book to take that into account. Make sure you go at the pace of the slowest member and choose a walk with an exciting objective in mind, such as a cave, river, waterfall or picnic spot. Many of the walks can be shortened to suit – suggestions are included at the end of the route description.

Dogs

Sheep or cattle may be found grazing on a number of these walks. Keep dogs under control at all times so that they don't scare or disturb livestock or wildlife. Cattle, particularly cows with calves, may very occasionally pose a risk to walkers with dogs. If you ever feel threatened by cattle, you should let go of your dog's lead and let it run free.

Enjoying the countryside responsibly

Enjoy the countryside and treat it with respect to protect our natural environments. Stick to footpaths and take your litter home with you. When driving, slow down on rural roads and park considerately, or better still use public transport. For more details check out www.gov.uk/countryside-code.

The Countryside Code

Respect everyone
- be considerate to those living in, working in and enjoying the countryside
- leave gates and property as you find them
- do not block access to gateways or driveways when parking
- be nice, say hello, share the space
- follow local signs and keep to marked paths unless wider access is available

Protect the environment
- take your litter home – leave no trace of your visit
- do not light fires and only have BBQs where signs say you can
- always keep dogs under control and in sight
- dog poo – bag it and bin it – any public waste bin will do
- care for nature – do not cause damage or disturbance

Enjoy the outdoors
- check your route and local conditions
- plan your adventure – know what to expect and what you can do
- enjoy your visit, have fun, make a memory

SHORT WALKS CORNWALL – FALMOUTH & THE LIZARD

ROUTE SUMMARY TABLE

WALK NAME	START POINT	TIME	DISTANCE
1. St Agnes Beacon and Wheal Coates	St Agnes Head	1½hr	4.5km (2¾ miles)
2. Portreath and Tehidy Country Park	Portreath seafront	2½hr	8km (5 miles)
3. Truro to Malpas and St Clement	Boscawen Park, Truro	2hr	5.5km (3½ miles)
4. Gwennap Pit	Fore Street, Redruth	2hr	5km (3 miles)
5. Carn Brea	Carnkie	2hr	5km (3 miles)
6. Trelissick and Roundwood Quay	Trelissick Garden	2hr	7km (4¼ miles)
7. St Mawes and St Just-in-Roseland	St Mawes Quay	3hr	10km (6¼ miles)
8. Flushing to Mylor Churchtown	Flushing Quay	2½hr	8km (5 miles)
9. Falmouth beaches and Pendennis Point	The Moor, Falmouth	2½hr	9.5km (6 miles)
10. Roseland Ramble	Place Ferry landing stage	2hr	6.5km (4 miles)
11. Frenchman's Creek	Helford	1½hr	4.5km (2¾ miles)
12. Penrose and Loe Bar	Penrose Estate	2hr	5.5km (3½ miles)
13. Poldhu and Halzephron Cliff	Poldhu Cove	1½hr	5km (3 miles)
14. Cadgwith and the Devil's Frying Pan	Cadgwith	2½hr	7.5km (4¾ miles)
15. Lizard Point and Church Cove	The Square, Lizard village	2hr	6km (3¾ miles)

MAP KEY

HIGHLIGHTS
Coastal views, industrial heritage
Coastal views, woodland
River and city views, scenic village and pub
Countryside views, history
Panoramic views, industrial heritage
Estuary views, woodland, history
Coastal views, scenic church, optional ferry ride
Coastal views, marina, optional ferry ride
Beaches, history, urban walking
Coastal views, lighthouse, history, ferry ride
River and countryside views, woodland, historic pub
Coastal and countryside views, woodland, beach
Clifftop views, historic church, beaches
Coastal views, fishing villages, sea arch
Clifftop views, mainland Britain's most southerly point

SYMBOLS USED ON ROUTE MAPS

(S) Start point

(F) Finish point

(SF) Start and finish at the same place

 Waypoint

 Route line

MAPPING IS SHOWN AT A SCALE OF 1:25,000

DOWNLOAD THE GPX FILES FOR FREE AT
www.cicerone.co.uk/1173/GPX

Returning to the ferry (Walk 10)

INTRODUCTION

Path along Halzephron Cliff (Walk 13)

Cornwall has been attracting visitors in great numbers since the Cornish Main Line between Plymouth and Penzance opened in the 1860s, followed by the expansion of the motorway network to Exeter in the 1970s. This is understandable given that the 700km long Cornish coastline contains over 300 beaches, many of them deserted and containing swathes of golden sand lapped by turquoise sea. The Atlantic Ocean encourages perfect surfing waves towards Cornish shores, making it one of the best surf locations in the world, with places like Fistral Beach near Newquay hosting major international surfing competitions.

The south coast is known as the Cornish Riviera, its sandy beaches and seaside resorts interspersed with quaint fishing villages, whereas the north coast is exposed to stronger swells, creating rugged cliffs and sculpting rock stacks. Inland, reminders of Cornwall's industrial heritage are ever-present, with the iconic silhouettes of tin mine engine houses dominating the skyline. As most mining activity in Cornwall has long ceased, nature has quickly regained these areas, and long-forgotten tramways and access tracks now provide easy routes through this unusual landscape.

TV programmes such as **Poldark** and **Doc Martin** and the imagery created by authors like Daphne du Maurier and Rosamunde Pilcher draw tourists to the area in the summer months, but those looking to avoid the crowds can still find refuge along some of Cornwall's less-trodden paths.

Walking in Falmouth and The Lizard

Including both the north and south coasts, Falmouth and The Lizard is a paradise for walkers. Coastal walks are perhaps the main attraction but the wooded creeks of Carrick Roads and the industrial heritage of the Redruth and Camborne mining area offer surprisingly pleasant walking. The majority of the walks in this book make use of waymarked trails, often the familiar acorn of the South West Coast Path or yellow public footpath arrows. While there should be no real navigational difficulties, particularly on coastal sections where keeping the sea on one side is instruction enough, don't underestimate the undulating nature of the Cornish coast.

The walks in this book can be enjoyed year-round; the remnants of autumn storms leave the sea angry and tumultuous – perfect for a clifftop walk – and the crisp winter air hurries walkers towards welcoming historic pubs. Of course, outside of the main tourist season the chance of claiming the perfect spot to enjoy the view with a pasty is greatly increased. All the walks are circular or there-and-back routes, and for many there are options to shorten or lengthen the walk as desired.

Things to see

It's not just about cliffs and beaches in Cornwall; the small city of Truro and busy port town of Falmouth cater to retail and cultural needs. Walk 9 explores the bustling town centre of Falmouth and the fortifications defending the Fal estuary, and Walk 3 provides an excellent view of Truro cathedral.

The natural harbour of the Fal estuary and the various tributaries that

Fishing boats at Cadgwith Cove (Walk 14)

St Mawes harbour (Walks 7 and 10)

feed the deep, meandering channel between Truro and Falmouth are well worth exploring and feature in Walks 6 and 7. It would be an oversight to visit the area and not take at least one ferry trip – Walk 10 makes use of the tiny 12-person open boat between St Mawes and Place.

It is Lizard Point – not Land's End – that is mainland Britain's most southerly point, where the Atlantic Ocean meets the English Channel. Walks 14 and 15 explore this dramatic stretch of coastline. Walk 8 from Flushing is a favourite walk in the area, with the perfect combination of coast and countryside and an excellent cafe at the marina halfway along.

Travel

The Cornwall Main Line bisects the area, with railway stations in Truro, Redruth and Camborne. A branch line from Truro serves Falmouth. Buses do exist in Cornwall, but in common with other rural areas require careful planning. The major settlements such as Truro, Falmouth, Redruth and Camborne have good bus links, and even some of the more remote villages have small minibus-style services. Some of the walks in this book do need a car, but taxis are available if required. Several routes make use of the ferry network around the Fal estuary to access the more remote walks.

Where to stay

Falmouth makes an ideal base for exploring the area. As expected from a popular tourist destination there is a wide range of accommodation available in the area, from basic camping in farm fields converted for the summer, to stately hotels and self-catering cottages. There is even the option of staying in a lighthouse (Walk 10).

Towanroath Engine House at Wheal Coates

WALK 1
St Agnes Beacon and Wheal Coates

Start/finish	White Rocks car park, St Agnes Head
Locate	TR5 0NU ///ramp.dilute.rules
Cafes/pubs	Cafe at Chapel Porth Beach (500m off route)
Transport	Bus to St Agnes (1.5km from start)
Parking	White Rocks car park (height restriction)
Toilets	None on route. Seasonal toilets at Chapel Porth Beach on longer walk

Time 1½hr
Distance 4.5km (2¾ miles)
Climb 150m

A short loop taking in one of the most photographed sections of the South West Coast Path and a scenic viewpoint

A classic loop incorporating the dramatically sited Towanroath Engine House on the South West Coast Path, part of the iconic Wheal Coates mine complex. After easy walking along the coast path, the route moves inland to ascend St Agnes Beacon, a prominent local landmark and viewpoint. The ascent to the summit is steep but short-lived, with plenty of opportunities to stop and admire the coastal views.

View from St Agnes Beacon

SHORT WALKS CORNWALL – FALMOUTH & THE LIZARD

1 White Rocks car park is at the very southern end of the main **St Agnes Head** car park. Head along the South West Coast Path at the far end, with panoramic views along the coast to Porthtowan and Portreath with Godrevy Point and St Ives in the distance beyond. The walking is easy, with clear waymarking. There is an obvious capped mineshaft – turn right

Looking towards the Wheal Coates mine complex

at this point as directed and continue to follow the path. Towanroath Engine House comes into view, with the large Wheal Coates mine complex above. Turn right at the next junction to drop down to the engine house. Carry on for 500m to reach the cafe and toilets at Chapel Porth Beach.

2 Retrace your steps back along the coast path a short distance and take two consecutive right turns, the second time a sharp hairpin heading uphill towards the ruined **mine** buildings. Spend some time exploring the area, then head towards the intact chimney at the back of the site and pass to the left of it. The gravel path leads through a car park to reach a surfaced road.

3 Turn left along the road, then first right into **Beacon Cottage Farm**. Follow the track through the farmyard as signposted, then take a left fork, cross a field and pass through a stone stile. There are several paths here but try to remain on the most prominent path before curving left and uphill to reach the summit of **St Agnes Beacon**.

> ⓘ *During the Napoleonic War in the early 1800s, a guard was permanently stationed on the summit of St Agnes beacon.*

At 189m the summit offers panoramic views over the Cornish landscape and coastline, and a metal plate on the summit pillar shows

St Agnes Beacon summit pillar

places of interest. This prominent landmark has served as a burial and ceremonial site and more recently was a coastguard lookout-post and World War 2 radar station.

4 Continue over the summit mound and take the left-hand fork. Ignore any paths heading right, which eventually lead into St Agnes. Follow this rocky path downhill to reach a road.

− To shorten
Turn around at Towanroath Engine House and retrace your steps to the car park, shortening the walk by 1hr.

+ To lengthen
Continue along the South West Coast Path from Towanroath Engine House to reach Chapel Porth Beach, which has a cafe and toilets. From here a footpath returns inland to the Wheal Coates car park at Waypoint 2 to rejoin the main route. Adds 30min.

5 Cross the road, passing to the left of the parking area down a surfaced lane. After the sentry box turn left and pass through a metal gate. During World War 2 this area was the site of the 10th Light Anti-Aircraft Battery, with infrastructure including a chapel and garrison theatre. Go straight ahead to enter an area of heathland and continue in a straight line to return to the White Rocks car park.

Wheal Coates

The tin mine at Wheal Coates opened in 1802 and worked until 1889. The mine extended some distance under the sea, causing frequent flooding. Towanroath Engine House was built in 1872 to pump water from an adjacent 180m shaft. Other buildings on the site include two Whim engine houses, which were used to crush ore for processing, and a calciner used to roast the tin to remove impurities such as arsenic. At the peak of the mine's operation around 140 miners were employed at Wheal Coates.

Following easy trails in Tehidy Country Park

WALK 2
Portreath and Tehidy Country Park

Time 2½hr
Distance 8km (5 miles)
Climb 200m

A walk of contrasts – from the golden sands of Portreath across clifftop moorland to an elegant woodland estate

Start/finish	Portreath seafront
Locate	TR16 4NN ///airstrip.basics.juggled
Cafes/pubs	Several pubs and restaurants in Portreath, cafe at Tehidy Country Park at South Drive (500m off route)
Transport	Bus service to Portreath and Tehidy Eastern Lodge
Parking	Car parks in Portreath, Basset's Cove and Tehidy Country Park
Toilets	Portreath and South Drive in Tehidy Country Park

This circuit offers the best way to enjoy this part of the Cornish coast, combining panoramic views over a rugged seascape with easy walking in a mature wooded estate, the former seat of the mine-owning Basset family. The walk described here begins at Portreath but you can begin at any point on the circuit.

Looking back to Portreath

SHORT WALKS CORNWALL – FALMOUTH & THE LIZARD

1 From the seafront car park in **Portreath** turn right up the hill, then right again onto Battery Hill as it rises above the sandy beach, with **Gull Rock** visible just offshore. Follow the road as it drops down into a small bay dotted with houses.

Portreath was once an important port exporting copper. The Monkey Hut on the end of the pier once sheltered the harbour pilots who would wave flags or lanterns to guide ships into harbour. The white conical structure on the

WALK 2 – PORTREATH AND TEHIDY COUNTRY PARK

South West Coast Path waymarker above Porth-cadjack Cove

cliff above is known locally as the Pepperpot and was built in 1846 as an aid to shipping.

2 Watch for a coast path sign indicating the footpath towards **Western Hill**. Pass through the gate and immediately right to climb up onto the headland. The view east from here along the coast is spectacular, but don't get too close to the eroding cliff edge. Follow the path left (west) along heath-covered **Carvannel Downs** as it curves above the beach of Western Cove to the vast canyon known as Ralph's Cupboard. The ridge of rock and grass that projects from the cliff face and makes up the east wall is The Horse and is believed to be the remains of a collapsed cavern. Continue along the coast path, keeping the sea on your right to the start of a series of descending switchbacks.

3 The clear path switchbacks down and up **Porth-cadjack Cove**. Here 19th-century smugglers reputedly hoisted their contraband from the beach using an elaborate system of pulleys. The view along the coast

Mature woodland at Tehidy Country Park

towards Godrevy Lighthouse is spectacular and provides a good excuse for a breather. Reaching the car park at **Basset's Cove**, turn left along the access track to reach a road.

4 Cross the road and turn right along the verge to enter **Tehidy Country Park** at the North Cliffs car park. Head through the car park and along the wide avenue beyond. The mature woodland offers a real contrast to the open clifftop moorland left behind, with wide, easy paths. Turn left at the T-junction, then fork right at the next split. Turn left when the path reaches the woodland boundary at some houses and follow the main path. After 400m this path reaches a crossroads with a wooden signpost. A cafe and toilets can be reached by turning right here along the track for 5min.

> ⓘ *The Portreath Tramway transported copper ore from mines near Scorrier to Portreath harbour. Starting operation in 1809 it was the first railway in the county of Cornwall.*

5 Turn left, following the main gravel path signposted towards East Lodge. The trail forks right, then after 500m fork slightly left to follow a treelined avenue alongside a **golf course**. Branch left at the end of the golf course to reach a car park. Go through this to a road and cross where indicated onto a path signposted 'Mining Trail'.

> This path is one of the Mineral Tramways – a 60km network of multi-activity trails in Cornwall's central mining district, largely following the tramway and railway routes once used to transport tin and copper ore to the ports.

6 Follow the trail until it reaches a surfaced road at a crossroads. Continue straight ahead and down the hill adjacent to some holiday lodges and turn left. Watch for a path on the right through Feadon Wildlife Centre, then bear sharply left and follow a path down through woods to reach a surfaced road by Glenfeadon Castle (a holiday home). Turn left, pass beneath a bridge, then at a junction keep ahead along Tregea Terrace and back to **Portreath Beach**.

— To shorten
This route could be made linear by catching the bus back to Portreath from Tehidy Country Park. This would save 2km (40min).

✚ To lengthen
Continue along the coast path past Basset's Cove to enjoy more of the stunning coastal scenery.

The Basset family

The Basset family is believed to be descended from Osmund Basset of Normandy, who came over to England with William the Conqueror. The Tehidy Estate passed to the Basset family in the 12th century, and a large manor house was completed in 1863 by John Francis Basset, financed by revenues from tin mining. By 1870 income from tin mining was starting to diminish and in 1915 many of the Basset assets, including Tehidy, were sold off. In 1918 the manor house became a hospital for tuberculosis sufferers before burning down in 1919 and being rebuilt as Tehidy Chest Hospital. The estate was bought by Cornwall County Council in 1983 and became Tehidy Country Park.

Sunny Corner

WALK 3
Truro to Malpas and St Clement

Start/finish	*Boscawen Park, Truro*
Locate	*TR1 1SG ///task.youth.sports*
Cafes/pubs	*Cafe at Boscawen Park, pub in Malpas*
Transport	*Buses and trains to Truro, ferry service between Malpas and Falmouth via Trelissick*
Parking	*Car park at Boscawen Park*
Toilets	*Boscawen Park, Malpas and St Clement*

Time 2hr
Distance 5.5km (3½ miles)
Climb 140m

A wonderful, easy walk via the confluence of the Truro and Tresillian rivers to the pretty village of St Clement

This pleasant walk begins from the leafy outskirts of bustling Truro and provides an excellent alternative view of the cathedral. Follow the easy path to a tempting riverside pub and cross countryside on quiet lanes and footpaths to visit to the unspoilt village of St Clement tucked away on the Tresillian River.

The Heron Inn at Malpas

Confluence of the Truro River and Tresillian River

1 From the large free car park at **Boscawen Park** head towards the river and pass the tidal gates designed to protect Truro from flooding during particularly high tides. The riverside path winds past cricket and football pitches with the industrial area of Newham opposite. When the path joins Malpas Road, turn right along a very short section with no pavement to reach the moorings at **Sunny Corner**. The riverside path follows the road for a while before branching right to a seating area. Follow this, along the concrete quay and up a flight of steps towards the road. Don't go all the way – instead turn right onto a rough footpath through the trees. This path is pleasant, but a little rough in places. Reach a bench with a short flight of steps.

2 Go up the steps to join the road and turn right to follow the road into **Malpas**. There is no pavement but the road is quiet. The Heron Inn has a panoramic seating area overlooking the river and is the perfect place for a refreshment break. Continue along the road, passing the **marina** and ferry stop. As the houses begin to peter out, take a turning on the right signposted St Clement and turn immediately left to skirt above the houses along a driveway that soon narrows to a footpath, and enter woodland via a kissing gate. Keep right at the junctions, then drop down to cross two small footbridges and up to an iron kissing gate on the woodland boundary.

3 Enter the field and turn left before curving right and uphill. Go through a gate to the right of a large tree and follow the path as waymarked through the field boundaries, turning sharp left then right and dropping downhill with the church tower in view. The

WALK 3 – TRURO TO MALPAS AND ST CLEMENT

path becomes a lane and reaches a junction in the middle of **St Clement**. Continue straight ahead to reach the church in a small square next to attractive thatched cottages. From the church head back to the road and turn right, walking uphill to reach the St Clement noticeboard, then turn left, passing the village hall. Turn right then left to bypass the house and grounds at Druids Stitch on a narrow, overgrown footpath that soon opens out into a field. Cross the field, go through a gate onto a farm track and reach a surfaced lane.

4 Turn left along the lane then right onto a shaded path parallel to an access drive. Fork left along a gravel footpath and reach a small collection of barn conversions at **Park Farm**. Turn right to pass the buildings along a track, then turn right where indicated by a yellow waymark arrow and follow the field boundary downhill to a tall cedar tree. Here the path leaves the field to the right and runs downhill on a narrow path through woodland to a stile by a galvanised gate and eventually to **Malpas Road**. Turn right and follow the road back to Boscawen Park.

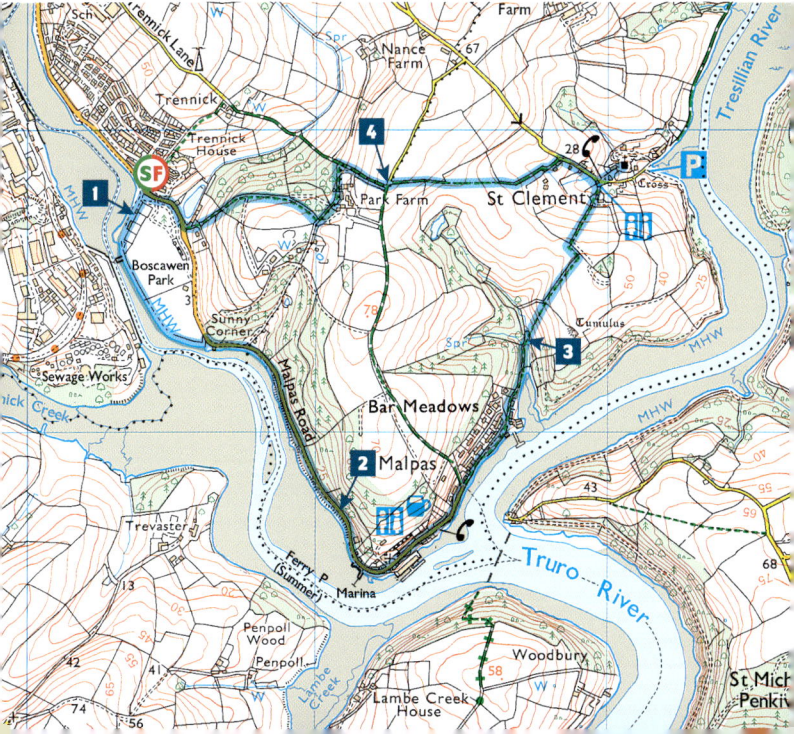

St Clement Church

> ### − To shorten
> In good weather the Heron Inn is a worthy destination in its own right, so after enjoying the views retrace your steps to Boscawen Park. This would save 3.5km (1½hr).
>
> ### + To lengthen
> Continue along the riverside path from St Clement to Tresillian, adding 2.5km (45min), and return to Truro via public transport. Or retrace your steps from Tresillian to rejoin the route at St Clement, adding 5km (1½hr).

Truro

Truro prospered in the 18th and 19th centuries as tin prices increased, and there were many cargo ships using Newham as their home port. As well as copper and tin exports, explosives from Nobel's factory in Perranporth were loaded on to ships there. From 1840 passenger boats operated between Truro and Falmouth, and in the 1860s a direct railway link to London Paddington was established. In 1877 Truro gained city status. Shortly afterwards work began on the Cathedral of the Blessed Virgin Mary, built to a Gothic Revival design. It was the first Anglican cathedral to be built on a new site in England since Salisbury Cathedral in 1220.

WALK 4
Gwennap Pit

Start/finish	*Cornish miner statue in Fore Street, Redruth*
Locate	*TR15 2BQ ///reported.minimums.stretcher*
Cafes/pubs	*Plenty of pubs and cafes in Redruth, farm shop at Grambler Farm*
Transport	*Train and buses to Redruth*
Parking	*New Cut car park (400m from start)*
Toilets	*New Cut car park*

Time 2hr
Distance 5km (3 miles)
Climb 100m

A linear walk from urban Redruth into the countryside to an open-air amphitheatre

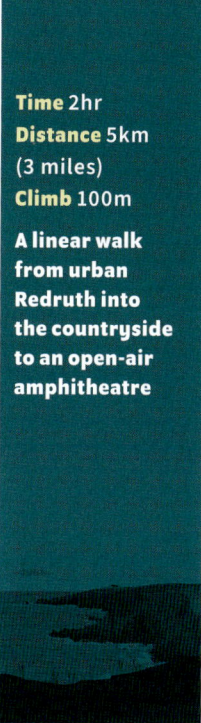

This linear walk leaves behind Redruth, centre of Cornish mining in the 19th century, to cross farmland and reach the impressive open-air amphitheatre of Gwennap Pit, made famous by John Wesley, the founder of Methodism in the 18th century. The timings above represent a there-and-back trip, but it could be completed one way making use of a taxi back to Redruth.

Country lane outside Busveal

Cornish miner statue in the centre of Redruth

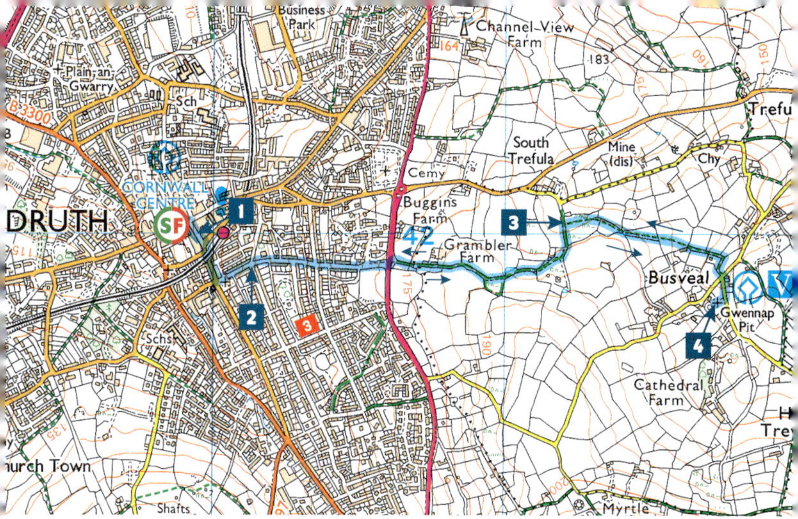

1 This walk begins from the bronze Cornish miner statue at the top end of the pedestrianised section of Fore Street. Facing the statue, turn right along Alma Place. Pass the library then turn right onto Station Road and head under the railway bridge on Bond Street. Go past Basset Street on the left then, at the Passmore Edwards building, turn left along Heanton Villas to pass St Andrews Church. Continue uphill to the crossroads.

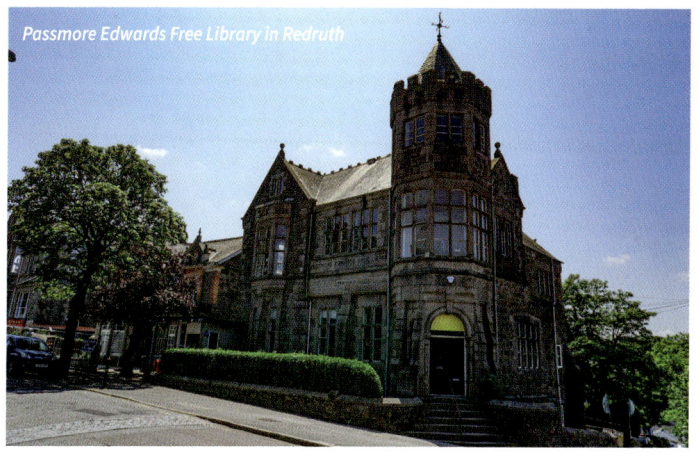
Passmore Edwards Free Library in Redruth

Interpretation panels at the entrance to Gwennap Pit

Gwennap Pit

WALK 4 – GWENNAP PIT

> ⓘ Murdoch House in Redruth was the first domestic residence in the world to be lit by gas, installed by engineer William Murdoch in 1792.

2 Head straight over onto Raymond Road. Eventually the A393 – known locally as Sandy Lane – is reached. Cross carefully and onto the lane opposite, which leads to **Grambler Farm**. Keep the farm buildings on your left (unless visiting the little farm shop) to enter a bridleway. This pleasant track winds through farmland. Keep left at the first and second fork, then as the landscape starts to open out watch for a footpath on the right heading into a scrubland area.

3 The footpath squeezes between two fields and over a stone stile to reach a farm track. Follow this access track as it turns right then reaches a surfaced road at **Busveal**. Turn right then immediately left to reach **Gwennap Pit**.

4 Spend some time enjoying the peace and tranquillity of the amphitheatre and associated chapel and museum before retracing your steps to **Redruth**.

> **— To shorten**
> Walk as far as Gwennap Pit and take a taxi back to Redruth.

Gwennap Pit

Gwennap Pit is thought to have been created when the surface collapsed into an abandoned mine below. On 6 September 1762 the principal founder of the Methodist movement, John Wesley, came to Gwennap, attracting a large crowd of tin miners. It was a particularly windy day and Wesley could not make himself heard at his usual location, so the whole crowd walked to the shelter of Gwennap Pit, about 2.5km away, and Wesley was able to preach his sermon. Wesley preached at Gwennap Pit 18 times between 1762 and 1789, and after his death the local people turned the pit into a regular circular shape with turf seats. Gwennap Pit is accessible at all times, but the neighbouring visitor centre and chapel are only open between Spring Bank Holiday Monday and 30 September.

Basset Monument

WALK 5
Carn Brea

Start/finish	*Carnkie*
Locate	*TR16 6RY ///thank.inversion.goes*
Cafes/pubs	*Pub in Piece*
Transport	*Occasional bus to Carnkie*
Parking	*West Basset Stamps car park behind 1 Post Office Terrace*
Toilets	*No public toilets on route*

Time 2hr
Distance 5km (3 miles)
Climb 120m

A hill walk with a surprisingly remote feel in the centre of the Cornish mining district

The great mound of Carn Brae is visible from most of the Redruth and Camborne area, surmounted by a castle-shaped stone folly and obelisk looming over the surrounding landscape. This walk begins from West Basset Stamps, a complex built in 1875 to process the ore produced by nearby West Wheal Basset Mine, with a tramway connecting the two. If you explore the site, you'll find a particularly fine example of a 19th-century tin dressing floor.

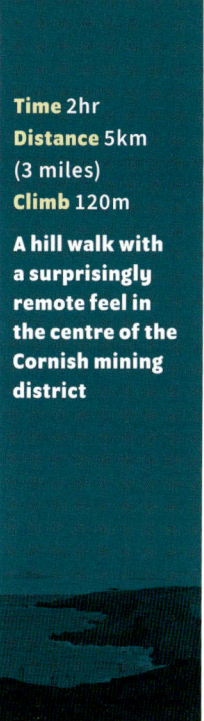

Redruth seen from Carn Brea

North Wheal Basset Engine House

WALK 5 – CARN BREA

1 Park in the small car park behind 1 Post Office Terrace, following the track next to the post box. Right next to the car park is Lyle's Shaft and Pumping Engine House, part of North Wheal Basset Mine. After exploring this, head back to the main track and turn right to continue north east. The track soon passes the overgrown ruins of West Wheal Basset Stamps. These can be accessed via one of the small paths heading left off the track and are well worth a diversion. Back on the main track, the views open up to the right over farmland, with a succession of engine houses on the horizon. Ignore tracks heading off left and right until the track narrows to a footpath, then take the second of two footpaths heading left and uphill.

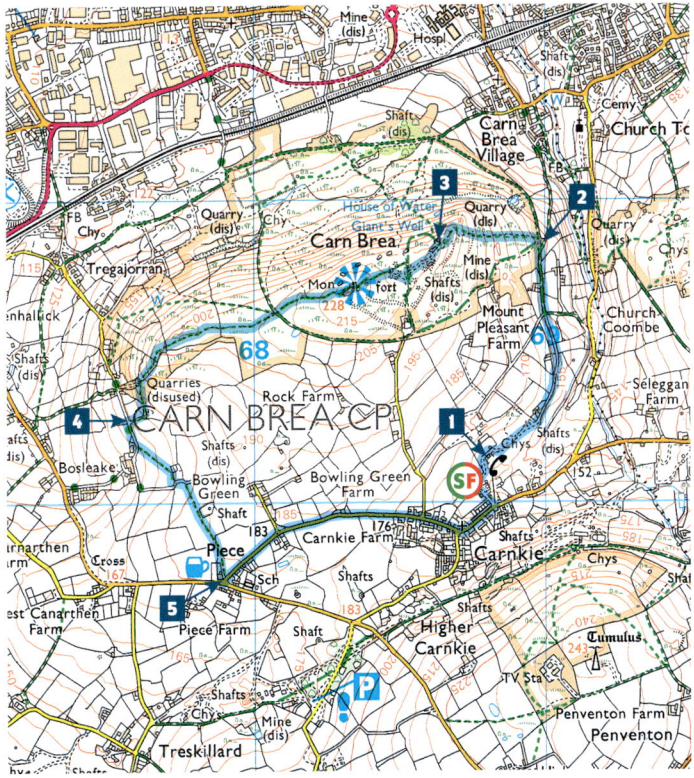

Carn Brea Castle

2 This path winds slowly past a series of rocky tors, providing increasingly good views over Redruth and the northern coastline, to reach **Carn Brea Castle**.

Carn Brea Castle was originally built as a chapel to St Michael around 1379 before being converted to a stone folly by the Basset family in 1790 and used as a hunting and feasting lodge. It is now a restaurant.

ⓘ *The Cornish flag, the black-and-white flag of St Piran, represents white lines of tin between dark molten rocks.*

3 Continue past the castle along the road with the obelisk of the **Basset Monument** ahead. At a small parking area branch right onto a footpath leading to the monument. The 28m high hexagonal column was erected in 1836 and contains a staircase leading to a viewing platform, though the access gate is usually locked. Pass to the left of the monument and curve

WALK 5 – CARN BREA

> ⓘ *The traditional Cornish language is known as Kernewek. It is part of the Celtic language family and was declared extinct in 1777. Recently Kernewek has been making a revival.*

right before some rocky outcrops then left to pick up a footpath continuing south west along the ridge. Continue to trend left as the path descends to a T-junction.

4 Turn left at the junction onto a narrow footpath. Before reaching **Bosleake** cross the wooden stile on the left into a meadow and follow the path uphill to a stile and gate. Cross this, go along a narrow path and turn left along a track. Cross a stone stile on the right and into a field, passing a large, capped mineshaft to reach a further stile. Go over the stile and follow the field boundary to meet the road by The Countryman Inn in the hamlet of **Piece**.

5 Turn left and follow the minor road back into **Carnkie** and the car park.

> **– To shorten**
> From Waypoint 3 follow the access road for Carn Brea Castle downhill to reach the minor road West of Carnkie. Turn left to follow this back to the car park. Saves 2km (45min).

West Wheal Basset Stamps

This complex was built in 1875 to accommodate the increasing demand for tin ore processing from West Wheal Basset Mine. Stamps are heavy metal weights that are lifted and dropped onto ore by a crankshaft, before further processing of the crushed ore through Frue vanners, shaking tables that separated black tin from other materials. There are two calciners on the site, where the tin ore was roasted to remove arsenic, an impurity in the tin which could be sold on as a valuable by-product. The machines at West Wheal Basset Stamps were powered by steam-driven engines requiring a supply of water drawn from a shaft at the rear of the engine house.

View over Lamouth Creek

WALK 6
Trelissick and Roundwood Quay

Start/finish	Trelissick Garden, near Truro
Locate	TR3 6QL ///beside.training.yummy
Cafes/pubs	Cafe at Trelissick Garden
Transport	Bus to Trelissick Garden
Parking	Trelissick Garden car park (National Trust)
Toilets	Trelissick Garden, opposite the gift shop

Time 2hr
Distance 7km (4¼ miles)
Climb 150m

Explore the woodland and creeks surrounding the stately Trelissick Estate

A dog-friendly stroll exploring the peninsula that makes up the Trelissick Garden estate. Easy wooded trails above creeks and the wide expanse of the River Fal lead to the Iron Age promontory fort and historic Roundwood Quay, once a hive of activity but now a quiet spot to relax and enjoy a picnic.

River Fal

SHORT WALKS CORNWALL – FALMOUTH & THE LIZARD

1 From the car park at **Trelissick** head through the gate and cross the cattle grid to enter the parkland. The views across the Carrick Roads river estuary are already impressive, but make your way straight ahead and head downhill towards the shore and the panorama will begin to open out. At the bottom of the hill turn left through a gate to pass above the beach and follow the path to a gate labelled 'Woodland Walk'.

> ⓘ *As the most southwesterly region in the UK, Cornwall is on the eastern edge of the Gulf Stream so enjoys a mild maritime climate.*

WALK 6 – TRELISSICK AND ROUNDWOOD QUAY

2 Go through the gate and stride out along the easy track as it curves north to follow the ponderous **River Fal** upstream. Eventually you will reach a flight of steps dropping down to the road. A short distance downhill is the King Harry Ferry, a chain link ferry established in 1888 to connect Feock with the Roseland Peninsula. Cross the road and go up the steps on the other side.

3 Follow the wooded track as it curves left and leaves the Fal estuary behind to shadow muddy **Lamouth Creek**. At the head of the creek ignore the path branching left (you'll return to this point later), and in a short distance turn right to cross a wooden footbridge.

4 Follow the path as it curves right, ignoring any paths forking left to remain alongside the shoreline. In a while a National Trust marker for Round Wood is passed. Stay on the main track to pass through the earthworks of the Iron Age fort and drop down a flight of steps to reach Roundwood Quay.

River Fal from Roundwood Quay

The quay was a hive of industrial activity in the early 18th century, accommodating ships of up to 300 tons transporting copper and tin ore from the Chacewater and North Downs mines. There is also evidence of a lime kiln and copper smelting facility.

> ⓘ *Since 2011 the Cornish pasty has enjoyed protected status, so a pasty can only be considered a 'Cornish' pasty if it was created in Cornwall.*

5 Retrace your steps to the wooden footbridge, this time keeping Lamouth Creek on your left. Cross the footbridge and turn left, then right up a winding track through **Namphillows Wood**, making use of a particularly scenic bench en route. The track eventually reaches a gate at a surfaced road. Cross carefully and re-enter the estate at the Old Lodge. Take the right fork after the lodge, then left to cross the cattle grid and into the open parkland. Follow the wide track to a gate and cattle grid and back to the car park.

> **— To shorten**
> Cut out the section to Roundwood Quay by turning left at Waypoint 4 to follow the zigzag path uphill through the woods to Old Lodge, saving 2km (40min).

Trelissick House

Erected by John Lawrence in the 1750s, Trelissick passed to the wealthy Daniell mining family in the 1800s. When Thomas Daniell became bankrupt through gambling, the house was sold to help pay off his debts. Eventually the estate ended up in the hands of Carew Davies Gilbert, who was a major Victorian plant collector and contributed hugely to the development of the garden. From 1937 the house was owned by Ida Copeland, who was married to Ronald Copeland, chairman of the Spode Copeland china works. The Copeland family used Trelissick House as a summer home until it was given to the National Trust, with the house and walled garden being retained as a family home.

WALK 7
St Mawes and St Just-in-Roseland

Start/finish	*St Mawes Quay*
Locate	*TR2 5DG ///sleepy.paint.scratches*
Cafes/pubs	*Several pubs and restaurants in St Mawes, cafe at St Just Church*
Transport	*Passenger ferry to St Mawes from Falmouth or seasonal ferry from Place Creek on the Roseland Peninsula. Bus service to St Mawes and St Just-in-Roseland*
Parking	*Car parks in St Mawes and by St Just Church*
Toilets	*St Mawes car park and St Just Church*

Time 3hr
Distance 10km (6¼ miles)
Climb 200m

A varied circuit from the historic fishing village of St Mawes to one of the most picturesque churches in Cornwall

This walk can easily be combined with the scenic ferry from Falmouth to St Mawes, which takes 20min and gives an alternative view of historic Falmouth. Much of the route offers views over Carrick Roads, before turning inland at the beautifully situated St Just-in-Roseland Church for a panoramic high-level stroll back to St Mawes.

St Mawes

WALK 7 – ST MAWES AND ST JUST-IN-ROSELAND

1 From St Mawes quay turn left (west) and follow the seafront road as it curves towards **St Mawes Castle**.

> This four-storey artillery fort was built on the orders of Henry VIII between 1540 and 1542. Together with Pendennis Castle, visible across the water, it protected Carrick Roads from French attack.

Pass above the castle and follow the minor road along the coast past some houses. The surfaced road ends at a gate, signifying the start of National Trust land.

2 Follow the coastal footpath as it curves north, enjoying the views across **Carrick Roads** to Trefusis Estate and Mylor Churchtown. There are several opportunities to drop down to secluded beaches on the left or to return to St Mawes by turning right, but otherwise remain on the main footpath through a sequence of gates and over stiles. Cross a wooden footbridge, then at the end of the footpath turn right then left and follow the path to Pasco's Boatyard. There has been a boatyard here since the Pasco family leased the land 1771.

3 Pass the boatyard buildings and follow the clear signs to turn right onto a narrow path above the dinghy racks and shingle foreshore. This pleasant path offers views over tranquil **St Just Creek** and soon opens out as it enters the churchyard of St Just-in-Roseland Church. This has to be one of the most beautifully located churches

St Just-in-Roseland churchyard

SHORT WALKS CORNWALL – FALMOUTH & THE LIZARD

St Just-in-Roseland Church

in the country, offering a haven of peace and quiet and the perfect place for a pause.

4 Follow the path rising steeply behind the church, head through the lychgate and emerge at a road. Turn left then almost immediately right up a small flight of steps. The path winds uphill to the right to reach the start of National Trust land at **Church Town Farm**. Cross the stile and follow the easy path, with panoramic views over Carrick Roads to Falmouth. Just before you reach the A3078 road look right for a stile entering a field. Cross this and enjoy the easy walking towards a water tower. Pass to the left of the tower, walk alongside the road for a short distance, then cross over onto a path through Voskelly Farm. Alternatively you could continue straight ahead along Polvarth Road and Hillhead to return directly to St Mawes.

Percuil River

5 Continue through the buildings, curve right, then left and right again and descend to the gate for **Bosloggas**. Take the wooded footpath on the right and follow this – muddy in places – to reach the **Percuil River**. The path turns right here and continues south alongside the river to reach the outskirts of **St Mawes** at Freshwater Boatyard. Pass behind the yard buildings as directed and look for the footpath on the left which continues above the shore to reach Polvarth Boatyard. Turn right and follow the lane uphill to the road. Turn left along the pavement to return to the start.

> **− To shorten**
> You could shorten the circuit at Waypoint 4 by walking 500m to St Just-in-Roseland and making use of public transport to return to St Mawes. This saves 5km (1½hr)
>
> **+ To lengthen**
> This walk could easily be combined with Walk 10 by making use of the Place Ferry from St Mawes to the Roseland Peninsula.

King Henry VIII's Device Forts

St Mawes Castle

Both St Mawes and Pendennis castles were built as part of Henry VIII's Device Forts, a nationwide order or 'device' designed to defend the coast of England and Wales against French and Spanish attack. Defences ranged in size from small blockhouses to full stone castles. This programme of works took place between 1539 and 1547 and was largely funded from the proceeds of the Dissolution of the Monasteries a few years earlier.

View across to Falmouth from Flushing

WALK 8
Flushing to Mylor Churchtown

Start/finish	*Flushing Quay*
Locate	*TR11 5TY ///lions.snacks.lights*
Cafes/pubs	*Pubs and restaurant in Flushing, cafe at Mylor Yacht Harbour*
Transport	*Passenger ferry to Flushing from Falmouth. Buses to Flushing and Mylor Bridge (1km off route)*
Parking	*Very limited parking at Flushing Quay or the eastern end of Trefusis Road*
Toilets	*Prince of Wales Pier (Falmouth), Mylor Yacht Harbour*

Time 2½hr
Distance 8km (5 miles)
Climb 200m

A ferry ride and a classic circular walk with views across Carrick Roads

This straightforward route is ideally reached via a 10min crossing on the little passenger ferry from Falmouth's Prince of Wales Pier, which weaves through the moorings of Falmouth harbour. From Flushing Quay the walk wanders past stately houses of packet ship captains onto the coastal path through Trefusis Estate to reach the marina at Mylor Churchtown. The return route follows Mylor Creek before heading inland through pleasant woodland.

The Flushing ferry

WALK 8 – FLUSHING TO MYLOR CHURCHTOWN

1 From **Flushing Quay** head inland, passing The Waterside restaurant, and turn right then left along a cobbled lane between rows of elegant houses. Head right along Trefusis Road as it winds past the former homes of packet ship captains and merchants, reaching Flushing Sailing Club.

2 The road curves left and uphill, then ends at a gate at the boundary to Trefusis Estate. Pass through the pedestrian entrance. A short detour right leads to a pleasant sandy beach with views over Falmouth. Continue past the Pilot Gig Club and Kiln Quay House as the surfaced road becomes a footpath which rounds **Trefusis Point** to run alongside Carrick Roads. Between

> ⓘ Falmouth was the finish line for Robin Knox-Johnston, who in 1969 was the first person to sail non-stop around the world single-handedly.

Trefusis Point and **Penarrow Point** there are numerous opportunities to access the rocky foreshore, though most require a bit of a scramble.

The surefooted and adventurous may be able to find a series of five steps cut into the rock, reputed to have been used by smugglers to bring contraband ashore, possibly via a nearby cave and tunnel to Trefusis House.

St Mylor Church and war memorial

Farmland on the Trefusis Estate

There are a few easy stiles as the grassy path curves left and skirts farmland to reach Restronguet Sailing Club. If tidal conditions allow you may prefer to drop down onto the beach to fully appreciate the views.

3 Further along, the large **marina** forming Mylor Yacht Haven has a cafe and toilets. Just past the main marina buildings, a pedestrian gate on the left takes you to the Church of St Mylor, which gives **Mylor Churchtown** its name.

> From 1866 to 1899, Mylor Churchtown housed training ship HMS *Ganges*, preparing around 14,000 boys for service in the Royal Navy. A memorial to 53 boys who died during training can be found in the churchyard.

4 Exit the churchyard via the upper gate, pass the war memorial and cross the road onto a surfaced lane. This lane descends to join pretty **Mylor Creek**. Continue along, the lane, with glimpses of the creek between the houses, to the small cove at **Trelew**. The 77-ton ketch Hobah was built here in 1878 and the information board is well worth a read. Continue up the road for a few more paces and turn left along the track to Trelew Farm. Just before you reach the buildings, divert left as indicated and enter a pleasant stretch of woodland which winds uphill to reach a surfaced road. Turn left to a crossroads and continue straight ahead to re-enter Trefusis Estate along a lane.

5 Go along the lane then turn right just before the first building and follow the footpath to a stile. Cross, then

turn immediately right to follow the field boundary downhill to another stile on the outskirts of **Flushing**. Follow the lane to reach a short flight of steps onto Kersey Road. This quiet road leads downhill, passing the Royal Standard pub on the corner. Turn left onto Trefusis Road, pass the Seven Stars pub and return to the quay for the return ferry to Falmouth.

− To shorten
Retrace the route from Mylor Churchtown to Flushing, saving 1km (20min).

+ To lengthen
Carry on along Church Road from Trelew into Mylor Bridge, returning to Trelew to continue the route. Adds 3km (1hr).

The Falmouth packet ships

Falmouth was appointed a packet station by Royal Mail in 1688 and had a fleet of sailing ships to carry messages to and from the far reaches of the British Empire. Falmouth packet ships often carried gold bullion, private goods and passengers as well as mail, but were lightly armed and relied upon speed to stay out of trouble. For over 150 years, until the age of steam, the harbour would have been filled with the hustle and bustle of sailing ships loading and unloading.

Street in Falmouth

WALK 9
Falmouth beaches and Pendennis Point

Start/finish	*The Moor, Falmouth*
Locate	*TR11 3QA ///glad.heap.shade*
Cafes/pubs	*Pubs and restaurants in Falmouth, cafes at Gyllyngvase and Swanpool beaches*
Transport	*Most local buses stop at The Moor, Falmouth*
Parking	*The Moor or Town Quarry car park, or park and ride during the summer*
Toilets	*Several passed in town centre, also at Castle Beach, Gyllyngvase Beach and Swanpool Beach*

This route shows the very best of Falmouth – with bustling streets giving way to wooded tracks and scenic viewpoints. There's the opportunity to enjoy two sandy beaches, perfect for a swim, and plenty of cafes and shops along the way.

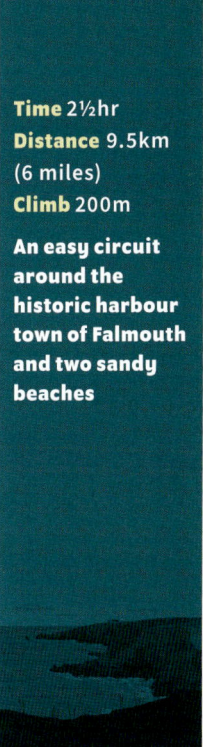

Time 2½hr
Distance 9.5km (6 miles)
Climb 200m

An easy circuit around the historic harbour town of Falmouth and two sandy beaches

Aerial view of Pendennis Castle

1 From The Moor, formerly an area of marshy ground drained in the early 19th century, head past the Passmore Edwards building that houses the library and art gallery and along Webber Street. Turn right then left onto **Prince of Wales Pier**, departure point for many tour boats as well as passenger ferries to neighbouring communities along Carrick Roads. This pier was opened in 1906 as an addition to the existing granite working quay.

2 Leave the pier and head along Market Street, Falmouth's main shopping street, with plenty of eclectic independent shops and cafes. At The Grapes Alehouse, where Market Street turns into Church Street, turn left and drop down to **Fish Strand Quay**. The quay was previously the site of Falmouth Gas Works, ensuring Falmouth became the first Cornish town to be lit by gas in the early 19th century. Follow the waterside to the

far end of the car park and negotiate a narrow alleyway returning to Church Street.

3 Turn left and follow the street as it curves left to pass the church of King Charles the Martyr. The road narrows as it becomes Arwenack Street before opening out again by the Trago Mills discount store and Custom House Quay, the oldest in Falmouth. Further along pass Discovery Quay.

This open-air arena and event space houses the National Maritime Museum Cornwall. On the right are the remnants of Arwenack House, once home to the powerful Killigrew family who founded Falmouth from 1661. Opposite sits the relocated Killigrew Pyramid, dating from 1737.

The Packet Quays and Greenbank Hotel from Prince of Wales Pier

Falmouth Docks

4 Continue along Marine Crescent and Bar Terrace to pass **Falmouth Docks**. The 30-hectare docks offer services to shipping, including the maintenance and refit of Royal Navy and Royal Fleet Auxiliary ships. Head under the railway bridge, over the roundabout, and uphill and left along Pendennis Rise. After around 300m a long layby provides a scenic viewpoint over the docks. Soon after fork left off the road onto the South West Coast Path, which winds through the trees with excellent views over Carrick Roads to St Mawes and St Anthony Head lighthouse. This easy path runs below Pendennis Castle to reach **Pendennis Point**.

> Now in the care of English Heritage, Pendennis Castle is one of several artillery forts commissioned by Henry VIII to defend Carrick Roads from invasion. Pendennis Point often offers the opportunity for an ice cream while admiring distant views of the Roseland Peninsula, The Lizard, and the deadly Manacles rocks.

5 Continue along the good path above Castle Drive, with views over the bay towards Gyllyngvase Beach, and turn left along Cliff Road above Castle Beach.

6 An easy stroll above the shoreline brings you to **Gyllyngvase Beach** – make sure to glance back towards rocky Pendennis Point. Gyllyngvase – from the Cornish *an gillynn vas*, which means 'the shallow inlet' – is a classic golden sandy beach with a cafe and takeaway. Continue along the South West Coast Path at the far end of the beach as it heads uphill above a rocky foreshore.

7 This footpath follows the coast before descending to **Swanpool Beach**. Head inland along the pavement alongside Swanpool Lake. The freshwater lake was cut off from the sea in the Ice Age and is now a Local Nature Reserve, home to a wide variety of bird species. At the far end of the lake turn left along Silverdale Road, then almost immediately left again. Look for a small road on the

Castle Beach and Gyllyngvase Beach

right which leads to a footpath entering Swanvale Nature Reserve. Follow the path through the woodland and turn right, leaving the woods at a residential area.

8 Follow the path through the residential area. Pass Marlborough House on the right, then continue onto Marlborough Avenue and under the railway bridge. Stay on quiet Marlborough Avenue until it reaches the main road at Western Terrace. Turn left, cross at the pedestrian crossing and descend back to The Moor along Killigrew Street.

> **— To shorten**
> You could shorten this circuit by returning to The Moor after Gyllyngvase Beach along Gyllyngvase Hill and Melvill Road, saving 1.5km (30min), or miss out Pendennis Point by heading straight on along Castle Drive instead of turning onto Pendennis Rise, and rejoin the route at Waypoint 6, saving 2.5km (1hr).

Falmouth harbour

Combined with Carrick Roads, Falmouth harbour is one of the largest natural harbours in the world, and the deepest in western Europe. In 1805 the news of Britain's victory at the Battle of Trafalgar (and Admiral Nelson's death) was landed at Falmouth at Fish Strand Quay from the schooner HMS *Pickle*, and was taken to London by stagecoach. The journey to London took just 38 hours, at a time when the trip usually took a week to complete.

St Anthony Lighthouse

WALK 10
Roseland Ramble

Start/finish	Place Ferry landing stage
Locate	TR2 5EZ ///parks.scales.relations
Cafes/pubs	Plenty of pubs and cafes in St Mawes or Falmouth
Transport	Passenger ferry from St Mawes or Falmouth
Parking	St Mawes or Falmouth, or St Anthony Head car park (National Trust)
Toilets	St Anthony Head (seasonal), St Mawes car park

Time 2hr
Distance 6.5km (4 miles)
Climb 200m

Take the tiny Place Ferry to discover the quiet Roseland Peninsula

The Place Ferry from St Mawes weaves through the moorings to land at a remote jetty on the Roseland Peninsula – the perfect start to this scenic coastal walk, though it can be quite an experience in a swell. You could also catch the ferry from Falmouth, changing at St Mawes, and a discounted combined ticket called the Roseland Ramble is available. If a ferry trip does not appeal, begin this walk from the National Trust car park at St Anthony Head, a short distance from the ferry landing.

On St Anthony Head

Place House

1 From the Place Ferry jetty, turn right along the obvious footpath and follow it to reach the gates of **Place House**. Continue straight on then take a footpath on the right over a stone stile.

This leads into the churchyard of St Anthony's Church, extensively restored in the 19th century but remaining a superb example of what a parish church was like in the 12th and 13th centuries. The churchyard contains an unusual medieval granite coffin.

Continue past the church door, up the steps and curve right, with Place House now on the right. Follow an easy track past **Cellars Beach** then into a sloping field containing two trees.

South West Coast Path through farmland

WALK 10 – ROSELAND RAMBLE

2 Follow the path uphill to reach a scenic viewpoint over Falmouth and Carrick Roads, with the twin castles of Pendennis and St Mawes in view. Take the path sloping downhill to the right towards the shore and follow it through a patch of pinewood at **Carricknath Point**. Follow this undulating path into a field. A path runs down to sandy Great Molunan Beach, worth a stop at low tide.

Continue along the main path to reach a wooden footbridge, cross and head up the steps.

3 Turn right and go through the gate to enter National Trust land at **St Anthony Head** and pass the former lighthouse paraffin store on the right. Follow the path ahead to drop down to the St Anthony Lighthouse.

Heading towards Porthbeor Beach

Built in 1835, the St Anthony Lighthouse featured in the introduction to the UK version of the TV puppet show *Fraggle Rock*. It remains an operational lighthouse, though the attached cottage is now a holiday let.

Turn around and head back up the slope, turning right at the fork and following the path up to the National Trust car park and holiday cottages. There's a path leading from the car park down to a bird hide that is worth a visit, especially when peregrine falcons nest on the opposite cliff face.

4 From the car park continue along the coast path with the sea on your right, passing a series of gun emplacements, with exceptional views over Falmouth and beyond to the Lizard peninsula. The path continues for another 2km before reaching the long flight of steps leading down to golden **Porthbeor Beach**. At the time of writing the steps down to the beach are closed due to a landslide.

5 From the steps head inland across the field to reach a kissing gate in the hedgerow. Pass through and turn right along the quiet road. Take the next left, signposted for **Bohortha**, and continue through the buildings. Ignore the junctions leading right and take a smaller, rough track straight ahead past the postbox. This narrows to a footpath, then turns right and into a patch of woodland. Emerge into a field above Place House, follow the path downhill and retrace your steps to the ferry landing.

> ⓘ At 34m deep Carrick Roads is the third deepest natural harbour in the world. It is only beaten by Sydney harbour and The Port of Mahon.

− To shorten
Turn around at St Anthony Head and retrace your steps to the ferry landing. The time for the walk is about the same, but this saves you some climbing.

+ To lengthen
Continue along the South West Coast Path from Porthbeor Beach to Porth Farm, head inland and follow the path along Porth Creek and the Percuil River to return to the ferry landing. This adds just under 3.5km (1hr).

St Anthony Battery

The concrete structures at St Anthony Head are the remains of a 19th-century gun battery built in 1895–97 to defend the River Fal estuary, though a battery of 24-pounder cannons were placed here in 1796 in response to an anticipated French invasion. The battery remained operational throughout both World Wars until it was decommissioned in 1956 and acquired by the National Trust in 1959. The former officers' quarters are now holiday cottages.

Helford village

WALK 11
Frenchman's Creek

Start/finish	*Helford*
Locate	*TR12 6JX ///lakeside.jetliner.loser*
Cafes/pubs	*Cafe in village car park, pub in Helford*
Transport	*Bus to Helford village car park. Seasonal passenger ferry to Helford from Helford Passage*
Parking	*Village car park at the end of public road to Helford*
Toilets	*In car park*

Time 1½hr
Distance 4.5km (2¾ miles)
Climb 160m

A relaxed circular walk along Daphne du Maurier's romantic creek

This gentle walk is to be savoured, with plenty of distractions en route, including the Shipwrights Arms and a secluded beach at Penarvon Cove. After enjoying panoramic views over the Helford River, drop down to the hidden, wooded creek before following an easy path through fields and woods back to Helford.

Leaving Penarvon Cove

Shipwrights Arms, Helford

1 From the large car park just outside **Helford**, follow the narrow road downhill past sleepy thatched cottages to a ford. Use the footbridge to cross, turn right and follow the road past the idyllically situated Shipwrights Arms pub, then turn left at the crossroads behind Poppygale Cottage. The path heading right leads to the passenger ferry across the river to Helford Passage. Turn right again on a public footpath leading through woodland to the beach at **Penarvon Cove**.

At the far side of the beach a path leads right and into Pengwedhen Wood. Keep right at the fork to reach a small memorial chapel dedicated to St Francis of Assisi. After visiting the chapel retrace your steps to the beach.

2 Follow the treelined road steeply uphill from the cove. At the top turn right along a gravel track as the views open out across fields and over the river. Descend gently towards the river, then turn left, continue downhill

WALK 11 – FRENCHMAN'S CREEK

> ⓘ *The name 'Cornwall' is thought to originate from the Cornovii tribe, meaning 'horn people', with horn referring to their location in the southwestern peninsula.*

and watch for a narrow path on the left with a National Trust sign indicating the route to **Frenchman's Creek**. Head down a few steps and into the ancient oak woodland.

Meadow at Kestle

3 An easy path meanders through the trees, offering glimpses of the quiet creek below. As the creek peters out, turn your back on it and head left uphill to reach a wider path. Turn left and follow the track as it passes beautiful wildflower meadows at **Kestle** to reach a surfaced road at a gate. Cross to enter the yard of Kestle Barton.

> Built in the 17th century on a medieval site first documented around 1300, the organic farm at Kestle Barton preserves precious habitats for a wide range of wildlife, and the barns have been converted into an arts centre.

> ⓘ *Cornish pasties are 'D' shaped, crimped on the side (never on top) and contain potato, swede, onion and beef with salt and pepper seasoning.*

4 Continue through the yard and out a gate into a meadow. Keep left along the field boundary and follow the path into woodland carpeted with fragrant wild garlic, snowdrops and bluebells in spring. Cross a stream and bear left to drop down into **Helford**. Follow the road uphill through the houses to return to the car park.

Helford village

Daphne du Maurier's Frenchman's Creek

Frenchman's Creek

Written in 1941, *Frenchman's Creek* by Daphne du Maurier is set in 17th-century Cornwall. The story follows Lady Dona St. Columb's journey to find excitement and escape from her privileged life. An encounter with the charismatic pirate Jean-Benoit Aubéry sparks a passionate affair, testing her commitment as a wife and mother. The novel artfully blends adventure, romance and societal constraints, delivering a compelling narrative that delves into themes of love, freedom and self-discovery.

Farmland near Penrose

WALK 12
Penrose and Loe Bar

Start/finish	Penrose Estate, Helston
Locate	TR13 0RB ///poetic.balance.shifts
Cafes/pubs	Cafe at The Stables, Penrose Estate
Transport	Bus to Penrose Hill just outside the car park
Parking	Penrose Hill car park (National Trust)
Toilets	The Stables, Penrose Estate

This walk begins with a stroll through the wooded Penrose Estate, in the care of the National Trust. The trails are wide and easy, offering views across Loe Pool, the largest freshwater lake in Cornwall. Drop down towards Loe Bar, a shingle bank which separates Loe Pool from the sea, then return across farmland to the car park.

Time 2hr
Distance 5.5km (3½ miles)
Climb 100m

Follow the path through Penrose Estate alongside Cornwall's largest freshwater lake to the shingle beach at Loe Bar

Easy track through the Penrose Estate

SHORT WALKS CORNWALL – FALMOUTH & THE LIZARD

1 Take the footpath at the far end of the car park next to the interpretive board, dropping down into the trees. Turn right along the estate track, then keep zigzagging downhill to pass the Tudor Gothic style bath house and well, with views opening up to Loe Pool. Turn right to reach The Stables cafe and walled garden.

WALK 12 – PENROSE AND LOE BAR

Loe Bar seen from Bar Lodge

2 Continue along the estate track, well waymarked with wooden signposts indicating Loe Bar. Ignore tracks heading inland and stay along the shoreside path. There are numerous benches en route providing opportunities to look out over **Loe Pool**.

> One condition of the gift of Penrose Estate to the National Trust in 1974 was that Loe Pool should be kept for people to enjoy without distraction – boating, swimming and fishing are not allowed.

Leaving the woodland, and with Loe Bar in view, the path curves right to pass **Bar Lodge**. It's possible to drop down to Loe Bar Beach from here, but heed the warning signs and don't enter the water.

3 At Bar Lodge turn around and take the path on the left sloping steeply back uphill. Zigzag uphill but keep right, ignoring paths heading left towards Porthleven. Heading inland, the path curves left and away from Loe Bar before reaching a T-junction. Turn right here along the gravel track. Skirting

> ⓘ In Cornish, a pasty is known as an Oggy. When cooked, the wives would shout 'Oggy, oggy, oggy!', and the men would shout back: 'Oi, oi, oi!'

farmland, reach a track just outside **Higher Penrose Farm**. Cross the track as indicated via a gate and follow the path as it bypasses the farm buildings, signposted for Penrose Hill car park. Just after the farm turn right along a wide gravel track to reach the car park.

+ To lengthen
Continue along the coast from Bar Lodge and explore Porthleven, then retrace your steps to Bar Lodge and continue the walk. This option adds 4km (1hr).

Loe Bar

Loe Bar

Loe Bar is a barrier beach, maintained by the deposit of shingle via longshore drift, with strong currents flowing south east from Porthleven to Gunwalloe. Though the bar is relatively porous, in the past water would occasionally back up in Loe Pool and flood Helston. The locals would have to break through the bar by cutting a channel, which would remain open until it naturally resealed. In 1780 an adit was constructed to prevent backflooding of the Castle Wary silver and lead mine at Nansloe, which was effective but required extending as the bar expanded in size. A concrete-lined adit with a sluice gate is used today to maintain the water level in Loe Pool.

The path along Halzephron Cliff

WALK 13
Poldhu and Halzephron Cliff

Start/finish	*Poldhu Cove, near Mullion*
Locate	*TR12 7JB ///stands.brotherly.cleans*
Cafes/pubs	*Cafe at Poldhu Beach and Church Cove*
Transport	*Bus to Poldhu Cove*
Parking	*Car park at Poldhu Cove*
Toilets	*Poldhu Cove and Winnianton Farm*

Time 1½hr
Distance 5km (3 miles)
Climb 125m

A walk along the coast to a medieval beachside church, followed by a dramatic clifftop path

A walk of two halves, this route follows the coast path between two sandy beaches before heading around the dramatic headland of Halzephron Cliff. Stop to admire the picturesque Church of St Winwaloe, which sits nestled in the sand dunes at Church Cove. The sandy, sheltered beach at Poldhu Cove is beautiful and is the perfect place to relax before or after this walk.

St Winwaloe Church

SHORT WALKS CORNWALL – FALMOUTH & THE LIZARD

1 Follow the lane heading uphill on the north side of the cove, enjoying the view back over the turquoise waters. Continue uphill and watch for the South West Coast Path forking off left – follow this around the headland, past a small car park and down into **Church Cove**.

2 Follow a sandy path across a footbridge and onwards to the idyllically located **Church of St Winwaloe** with its detached belltower.

St Winwaloe was a 5th-century Breton saint said to have founded the first church on this site. The current building dates from the 14th and 15th centuries and is the only church in Cornwall located on a beach. The exposed location has led to the church's nickname, The Church of the Storms.

3 Continue along the track to the buildings at **Winnianton Farm**. This is owned by the National Trust and

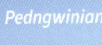
Pedngwinian

> ⓘ **The Chough** – pronounced 'chuff' – features in the county's coat of arms reflecting its importance in Cornish culture. There are around 350 breeding pairs in mainland Britain.

contains a small cafe, car park and toilets. Head through a gate to return to the South West Coast Path and continue uphill, taking the left-hand fork where there is a choice, to reach the fractured and dramatic headland of Pedngwinian. Now following the path along **Halzephron Cliffs**, enjoy the dramatic views over the long sand beach at Gunwalloe to Loe Bar and Porthleven beyond. Reach a surfaced road at a layby.

4 Turn right and follow this quiet lane downhill and back to the buildings at Winnianton Farm. Continue onwards towards the beach and retrace your steps to the car park at **Poldhu Cove**.

> **− To shorten**
> Turn around at Church Cove and retrace your steps to Poldhu Cove. This saves 3km (45min).
>
> **+ To lengthen**
> Continue onwards from Halzephron Cliff to Gunwalloe Fishing Cove, perhaps visiting the pub at Chyanvounder, then return to Waypoint 4 to continue the walk. This will add 2km (30min).

Beach at Poldhu Cove

The wreck of the St Anthony

The St Anthony (or Santo António) was a Portuguese cargo ship that foundered in a storm in Gunwalloe Bay on 15 January 1527, en route from Lisbon to Antwerp. The ship was the personal property of King John III of Portugal, the flagship of his fleet, and its cargo, which included copper and silver ingots, is estimated to be worth over £15 million today. Local tradition says that the large 15th-century screen depicting the Crucifixion in the Church of St Winwaloe was salvaged from the wreck. The exact location of the wreck was only discovered in 1981.

WALK 14
Cadgwith and the Devil's Frying Pan

Time 2½hr
Distance 7.5km (4¾ miles)
Climb 230m

A coastal walk exploring two picturesque fishing coves and a spectacular arch and blowhole

Start/finish	Cadgwith
Locate	TR12 7LD ///facelift.emotional.gradually
Cafes/pubs	Pub and cafe in Cadgwith Cove, several pubs and restaurants in Lizard
Transport	Bus to Ruan Minor (1km off route) or Lizard village
Parking	Car park on outskirts of Cadgwith
Toilets	Cadgwith Cove and Lizard (500m off route)

As they have done for centuries, the fishermen of Cadgwith Cove land their catch directly onto the shore, hoisting their boats from the water up onto the shingle beach. This walk starts in the picturesque village of Cadgwith and explores the natural blowhole known as the Devil's Frying Pan and a beautiful stretch of Cornish coastline, before heading inland at tiny Church Cove.

Walking along the coastal path towards Church Cove

WALK 14 – CADGWITH AND THE DEVIL'S FRYING PAN

Fishing boat at Cadgwith

1 From the car park just outside the village follow the footpath gently downhill past tiny St Mary's Church and past the thatched cottages to reach the beach at **Cadgwith Cove**. This is a practical, working environment in contrast to many beaches in Cornwall. Turn back inland and left up the hill, exploring the viewpoint of The Todden on the left if desired. Otherwise continue uphill and onto a footpath, part of the South West Coast Path and waymarked with an acorn. Weave through buildings then turn left and follow the path above the **Devil's Frying Pan**.

The Devil's Frying Pan on a calm day

This is a natural feature formed when the roof of a cave collapsed, leaving a hole. In winter storms the sea surges through the arch and appears to boil within the cave, with the central boulder resembling an egg in a frying pan.

2 Continue along the easy undulating footpath along the cliff with lovely coastal views. There are a number of stiles to cross, but otherwise navigation is straightforward, just keep the sea on your

Thatched cottages above Church Cove

> ⓘ The true roots of the name Lizard are unknown, but it could come from the Cornish **lys ardh**, which means 'high court'; or **lezou** which translates to 'headland'.

left. Drop down into the settlement of **Church Cove**, with its straggle of old fishermen's cottages around the slipway. Turn inland along the road, passing some beautiful thatched cottages, to reach St Wynwallow Church. Pass this and continue along Church Cove Road, then on the outskirts of **Lizard village** go right at a fork onto Cross Common.

3 Go along the road and as it bends sharp left, continue straight ahead onto a footpath beside a field track. This path winds through the farmland to a lane before **Trethvas Farm**. Turn left along the lane, pass to the right of the farm buildings and follow waymarkers up a couple of stone steps onto a raised section through farmland to reach a lane just short of **Gwavas Farm**.

4 Turn right past the farm and a camping field and follow the lane as it turns left then right to reach a cluster of buildings at **Prazegooth**. Turn left along Prazegooth Lane and follow this downhill via a series to zigzags to **Cadgwith Cove**.

WALK 14 – CADGWITH AND THE DEVIL'S FRYING PAN

➖ To shorten
There are two opportunities to turn back inland from the coastal path after the Devil's Frying Pan, picking up the minor road between Gwavas Farm and Prazegooth. The first saves 5.5km (2hr), the second saves 4.5km (1½hr).

➕ To lengthen
Take in more of the coastal views by continuing as far as desired along the coast from Church Cove towards Lizard Point. Return to Church Cove to continue the walk.

Cadgwith Cove fishermen

In 2021 three of the 17th-century buildings used by the Cadgwith fishermen were put up for sale. The buildings are used to store fishing equipment and process the catch, as well as housing an art gallery and shops selling fresh fish. They were offered to the parish council for £300,000, resulting in widespread media attention and a hugely successful Crowdfunder appeal. This has secured the buildings for the community and safeguarded the infrastructure required by the Cadgwith Cove fishermen to continue their way of life.

Cadgwith Cove

Signpost at Lizard

WALK 15
Lizard Point and Church Cove

Start/finish	The Square, Lizard
Locate	TR12 7NH ///yesterday.hotspots.heeding
Cafes/pubs	Several pubs and restaurants in Lizard, cafes at Lizard Point
Transport	Bus to Lizard
Parking	Car parks in Lizard village and at Lizard Point
Toilets	Lizard village and Lizard Point

Time 2hr
Distance 6km (3¾ miles)
Climb 200m

A clifftop walk around the most southerly point in mainland Britain to a rocky fishing cove

This easy walk makes use of good footpaths from the centre of Lizard to the dramatic and rugged headland of Lizard Point. Heading east, the route passes a lighthouse and winds over rugged cliffs and around isolated coves before turning inland and returning via quiet country lanes. Watch for the wireless station, site of the first wireless radio transmission in 1901.

Lizard Point

SHORT WALKS CORNWALL – FALMOUTH & THE LIZARD

1 From the large parking area right in the middle of Lizard village follow the lane to the left of the Top House Inn towards the Post Office. Pass to the left of the Post Office along Penmenner Road, where the tarmac soon runs out and becomes a rougher track. Take the bridleway straight ahead where the track turns sharp right and follow this narrow path towards the sea. At Pistil Meadow turn left and cross a wooden footbridge to join the South West Coast Path. Head up a flight of steps and onto a clifftop path offering easy walking to reach the collection of shops and cafes at **Lizard Point**.

> Lizard Point is the most southerly point in mainland Britain, so it's surprising that so many people are focused on Land's End to John O'Groats journeys. Particularly as John O'Groats isn't the most northerly point either!

2 Keep heading east along the coastal path to pass the **Lizard Lighthouse** complex, watching out for seals basking on the beaches in Housel Bay. Drop down towards **Housel Cove**, then ignore the path heading inland and continue past Housel Bay Hotel. The clifftop path makes for a prominent white building, the former Lloyd's Signal Station. After passing **Bass Point** and the Lizard Wireless Station, turn right through a gate and follow

WALK 15 – LIZARD POINT AND CHURCH COVE

93

Lizard Lighthouse

3 From **Church Cove** turn inland along the road, passing some beautiful thatched cottages, to reach St Wynwallow Church. Pass this and continue along Church Cove Road, then fork left onto Beacon Terrace, pass Lizard Argyle Football Club and return to The Square.

the path past the new lifeboat station to the cluster of buildings nestled in Church Cove. A small fleet of fishing boats still launch from here.

− To shorten
Follow Lighthouse Road back to Lizard from Lizard Point, saving 3.5km (1¼hr), or continue a bit further along the coast and turn inland at Housel Cove, saving 2.5km (50min).

+ To lengthen
Continue along the coast from Church Cove towards Cadgwith as far as desired, before retracing your steps and rejoining the route.

Marconi and The Lizard

The physicist and inventor Guglielmo Marconi chose Bass Point as the location of the Lizard Wireless Telegraph Station while staying at Housel Bay Hotel in 1900. Working in simple wooden huts, in January 1901 Marconi successfully received a radio transmission from the Isle of Wight over 290km away, proving that radio would work over the horizon – something which many people thought impossible. Lizard Wireless Station was the first coastal radio station to receive an SOS call when in 1910 the *Minnehaha*, aground off the Isles of Scilly, radioed for help.

USEFUL INFORMATION

Travel

Transport for Cornwall
www.transportforcornwall.co.uk

Go Cornwall Bus
www.gocornwallbus.co.uk

Cornwall by Kernow (First Bus)
www.firstbus.co.uk/cornwall

National Rail
www.nationalrail.co.uk

South Western Railway
www.southwesternrailway.com

Great Western Railway
www.gwr.com

Fal River Ferries
www.falriver.co.uk/ferries

Tourism organisations

Visit Cornwall
www.visitcornwall.com

Falmouth Tourism
www.falmouth.co.uk

Discover Redruth
discoverredruth.co.uk

Discover Helston
discoverhelston.co.uk

Visit St Agnes
visitstagnes.com

The Mineral Tramways
www.cornwall.gov.uk/environment/countryside
then click on 'Cycle routes and trails'

National Trust Cornwall
www.nationaltrust.org.uk/visit/cornwall

Weather and navigation

Met Office
www.metoffice.gov.uk

Windy
www.windy.com

Ordnance Survey
www.ordnancesurvey.co.uk

Further reading

Walking in Cornwall: 40 coast, country and moorland walks by Graham Uney (Cicerone, 2015)

Walking the South West Coast Path: National Trail from Minehead to South Haven Point by Paddy Dillon (Cicerone, 2021)

Frenchman's Creek by Daphne du Maurier (Virago Modern Classics, 2003)

© Phil Turner 2024
First edition 2024
ISBN: 978 1 78631 173 3

Printed in Singapore by KHL Printing using responsibly sourced paper
A catalogue record for this book is available from the British Library.

© Crown copyright and database rights 2024 OS AC0000810376
All photographs are by the author unless otherwise stated.

CICERONE

Cicerone Press, Juniper House, Murley Moss, Oxenholme Road, Kendal, Cumbria, LA9 7RL

www.cicerone.co.uk

Updates to this Guide

While every effort is made to ensure the accuracy of guidebooks as they go to print, changes can occur during the lifetime of an edition. Any updates that we know of for this guide will be on the Cicerone website (www.cicerone.co.uk/1173/updates), so please check before planning your trip. We also advise that you check information about transport, accommodation and shops locally. We are always grateful for updates, sent by email to updates@cicerone.co.uk or by post to Cicerone, Juniper House, Murley Moss, Oxenholme Road, Kendal, LA9 7RL.

Register your book: To sign up to receive free updates, special offers and GPX files where available, register your book at www.cicerone.co.uk.